Words of Emotion & Experiences

BY:

Denise Kollock

Acknowledges:

This is for everyone who believed in me with all of my poetry, and told me to keep pushing forward. My family, friends, and many other supporters. Thank you for everything. I really appreciate it!

Also, even though this is a poetry type of book, there will be also be little short scenarios & topics based on what I've been through. So, I hope you enjoy!

- Denise Kollock

Table Of Contents

First Experience

Saturday,
October 24th, 2015,
I've experienced something special,
The happiness overwhelming the entire
building,
A beautiful stunning wedding.
The color scheme was purple,
How it was set up was magnificent,
Purple table cloths,
Bottles of Martinelli's Sparking Apple
Cider,
A plant painted purple to its fullest,
The ceremony itself was just elegant,
Seeing my moms friend in her gorgeous
white dress,
Walking down the aisle,
Plus as well with the bridesmaids,
And the grooms & the flower girls,
Seeing her holding hands with her love,
The moments are becoming real,
Seeing both of them extremely happy,
Hoping their marriage will be the best.

The Moment

The day is here,
The wait is finally over,
At least for my mom & my sister.
I on the other hand,
Have to wait for another couple hours,
Which is absolutely dreading.
The random anxiety inside,
Making me feel nervous,
But also with excitement.
My dorm was all cleaned,
I just got out of my English class,
On a beautiful Wednesday from my
memory.
Also hung out with my friends,
To not only calm from the anxiety,
But to also ease the time being
productive.
Once I got a text from my sister,
I left back to my dorm,
And waited patiently.
As time went by,
Started to get more anxiety,
And nervous about what to expect.
However,
When I got another text from my sister,
I knew the surprise or wait was over.
The moment is here,
Where I ran & cried,
To see my mom, sister, but my dad
home.

Too Precious

Seeing his face,
The way he walks,
How he communicate with his friends,
Wow,
What a lovely dork,
He's so hilarious,
Yet so dumb,
It's quite funny,
Acting like idiots,
Gosh he's such a great guy,
My mind is going bizurrk,
But I doubt it,
If I'll be his,
So that ruins quite a bit,
Oh well,
He's still precious though,
Yet an idiot.

Oh Music

Music,
It's something we all enjoy,
Entertainment in a heartbeat,
Music can have such a special meaning,
It can have a message that can hit you at
home,
It could also be something or a feeling you
can relate to,
Or it can be something to dance to,
Music is a way for people to express
themselves,
The tastes of their music can sense how
they're like,
For example,
I listen to variety of music,
Alternative, Pop, Rock, R&B, Christian
Music, World, so many,
All of those genres of music describe me,
Plus as well with Techno & Dance,
Some people of course do have opposites
of genres,
Maybe they're more of the heavy metal,
It depends on who they are & how they
are.

Three Bands

Music inspires us all,

Depending on the singer or band,

Whether by who they are,

Or what their message is saying in their songs.

One Direction,

5 Seconds of Summer,

Cimorelli,

These three inspire me to the fullest.

One Direction,

Was five but now four amazing lads,

One from Ireland three from the UK,

Their music & personalities glow me up.

5 Seconds of Summer,

Four Aussie cuties,

All play instruments,

Music makes me hyped & inspired.

Cimorelli,

Six talented beautiful sisters,

Played instruments but still do,

Inspired to have much girl power.

These bands are amazing,

Inspired to be myself,

To be hyped,

They'll go far.

Where I'm From

I am from a city of quiet,

Where people don't live much in,

Yet still in the middle of nowhere.

Few friends live here,

Most in other towns near it,

At night it's dark & bizarre.

The desert is plain,

Joshua Trees mostly everywhere,

Only few stores located.

The city can be crazy,

Memories I've made there,

Something I won't forget.

The Escape

Sitting in class,
Wanting to run away,
Need to escape from this reality.

Drive to a magical place,
Somewhere calm & refreshing,
Where my mind can ease & feel fine.

A place with no stress,
No worries,
Fantasy coming to life.

Be free,
Enjoy yourself & time,
Before it gets too late.

The surprising escape,
The escape out of reality,
Escape out of undying pain.

Is It Bad?

Is it just me,

Or is it I'm getting to a certain point,

The point where I want to give up on love?

I mean,

I should of course be patient enough, you know?

But, what if the patience isn't helping one bit?

What if you don't find that special one?

To spend months, years, or to be with forever,

Who you can go to for anything,

To be there in comfort during a struggle,

Or making well balanced financial decisions,

To be the main support system through thick & thin,

So many questions & thoughts in my head,

Yet barely no answers,

My mind is confused,

What do I really want?

That's the question I'll keep asking myself.

Worry & Fear

I have no idea,
The thoughts in my mind,
Images & sights that are horrifying,
An issue deep inside I'm afraid to deal with.
Honestly, I don't know how to deal with it,
I'm afraid,
I am indeed scared,
None of this has happened to me.
Sometimes I want to disappear,
At times I don't want to go out,
Hiding would also be often in times like this,
Or even at one point to just even cry.
Trying to stay strong for my family,
Staying strong for my friends at home,
All of this insanity going on inside,
It's getting to me & I'm slowly breaking.
Trying to breathe normally,
However it's quite opposite,
Heart is racing faster & my body is shaking,
Stomach is churning not knowing what will happen.
People have different reactions,
Mine is in total worried & feared,
A reaction I should feel in this case,
Since it has happened before.
I am worried,
I have no idea how long this will take,
This is getting out of hand,
I just don't know anymore.

That Girl

The way she smiles,
How her smile can light up
anyones mood,
Her fun, caring personality,
Makes everyone be her friend.
On the inside,
She's shy & awkward,
Feeling empty & lonely,
Yet suicidal & self harmed,
She's not the typical girl,
Who'd wear make-up,
Sets trends for clothes,
Who's totally preppy.
Her life wants to be over,
She has no hope left,
Wanting to try more but can't.

Broken Emotions

People see me as the free spirit,
The one who makes everyone laugh,
Who's always there for anyone in need,
The girl who has the kind gentle heart,
Lately that hasn't been occurring with some parts.
Yes I do make everyone laugh but myself,
I'm always there for anyone in comfort but myself,
Pretending to be happy when I'm literally in pain,
Trying to survive the struggle of pain,
There's points where I don't want to stay strong,
Points where I just want to give up,
Or when I just want to say forget it.
My emotions,
I knew how to deal with it,
I knew how to take control when I get like this,
Out of the sudden I couldn't do it,
With how I'm feeling at the moment,
It feels so shattering,
Very fragile,
All of this is uncontrollable.
I've been saying that I need help,
But now coming to realize,
I'm used to the way I've been hurt,
People feel bad with what's going on with me,
It's just... I used to feel bad for myself,
Until the point where I'm constantly getting hurt,
I just say that I'm used to all the hurt taken place,
I'm used to being rejected socially,
Being taken advantage of,
Using me because of my looks,
I don't really get it or anything in general.

5th Grade

5th grade year,
10 year old me learned a lot,
Went through so many things,
I was getting bullied (it got really bad),
As well with not knowing who my friends are,
I'd always leave early from school,
Because I was "sick",
When really I was getting away from the bullying,
The teacher I had,
Made me into the person I am today,
Yes,
I might of done some dumb things,
But I really appreciate how she believed in me,
I guess during the time I didn't believe in myself,
I was also changing in how I acted,
Not only around my family,
But friends also,
And it was getting bad to the point where my mom noticed,
She wasn't happy with what was going on,
I want to thank my 5th grade teacher,
For believing in me,
I miss you so much,
And I want you to know,
That the person I am today of the good grades,
You are the reason.

A Year Without You (Friend Wise)

Dedication : To my friend Chris Shutter who passed away February 2014 due to suicide. This poem was written from a year he passed. To all of our friends, we love you & miss you so much Chris. Endure To The End. <3

A year since you've been gone,

Nothing is the same,

Everything seems strange,

All of this is odd,

You not being here,

Not being physically here on this Earth,

Still absolutely shocking & surreal.

We all love you,

We all miss you,

I cherish the little moments we had,

Those moments that I won't ever forget,

The guy who played his guitar around school,

The ultimate potential he had with his talent,

We miss you Chris,

We love you Chris,

I miss & love you Chris,

Your music will be in spirit with me always.

Grandma & Grandpa

Dedication : To my grandma who passed away on June 28, 2014 & my grandpa who passed away on October 12, 2005. I love you both! All of my accomplishments are for you! This is my message to them.

Grandma :

It's been over a year since you passed away, and I'm honestly still trying to process that you're gone. This is one of the toughest experiences I've dealt with in a while. But don't you worry, I am continuing to be strong & stay who I am, and following in your steps of hard-working. Having a faith and trusting the Lord that I'll be alright. I miss your preaching about the Word. It motivated me a lot. I love you Grandma so much, and what I'm doing is for you!

Grandpa :

A whole decade since you've been gone, and I'm as well still in shocked. You working hard for the family, and I love & appreciate that. It inspired me to continue working hard in school & what I love to do. I love you Grandpa sooo much, and I wish I had more to say to you before you left. All my accomplishments are for you.

Addiction

The many, many days trying to figure out what's the deal of even what in the actual is going on with me. Am I falling hardcore? Am I getting attached quickly? Am I falling for the right person? The many questions that pop into my head, it makes my mind go insane! What if I find nobody? What if I don't have a significant other? What if I end up being forever alone? These **"what if"** questions kill me tremendously. I wonder why when I do have crushes, why do I crush hardcore? These are questions I can't even comprehend myself. Maybe I think *"What if I have an addiction"?* The addiction of always wanting love. Whenever seeing a couple, you want to gag or even get jealous. Well... more of jealous, because the desperate need of a relationship like that. Ugh, this thought, I can't even really let this feeling that I have go. The feeling of love is something I'm sure as hell can't let go of. Maybe what I really have is an addiction. Just like cigarettes, when you try to quite, you can't, because they're that addicting. That's how I feel about love.

I'm Sorry

I'm sorry. I'm sorry for looking the way I am. I'm sorry that I act different ways around people. Whether it's around my family, friends, or even important people. I'm sorry that my outfit doesn't match. I'm sorry that I enjoy smiling. I'm sorry that I love to laugh. I'm sorry that my laugh sounds like a hyena. I'm sorry that I might be sarcastic. I'm sorry that I'm sassy & fabulous. I'm sorry that I'm quirky. I'm sorry that I'm very awkward around people. I'm sorry that I'm ACTUALLY being myself. I didn't know that it was contagious. Congrats, it's still making me relevant, because my name is in your mouth. I'm SO sorry that I have the self-confidence. I'm also SOOO sorry that I love my confidence about every little thing of myself. I'm sorry that I actually have a kind heart, and I care about everyone in my life that's important to me. That I show compassion in what I love, because that's something I "should" be sorry about. Oh wait, no. I shouldn't. I should be PROUD. You may not like me for who I am, that doesn't mean I give an ounce of a crap. Those opinions don't mean nothing on me. Hate or dislike all you want, but THAT won't hurt me. So to the lovely haters & dislikers in the world who despise me, continue on, but just know that none of the hatred will hit me at home.

Take Me

Bring me into your world,
Filled with determination & excitement,
With many accomplishments & success.

Take me into your thoughts,
Am I on your mind,
What future plans are in store?

The love life,
Will there be the one and only,
Is there going to be unconditional love?

Take me into your life,
Take me in your success,
Take me in everything you're doing.

Hope You Know

*Dedication: My first love, if he
ever reads this, I actually wrote
this during Senior Year, so I've
kept this in for a while, but now I
just gotta say this & let you
know this.*

You,
Certain person,
Him.
If you're reading this,
There's something,
Something I want to say.
No matter what,
Your actions & attitude at times,
You are really awesome.
Some of your actions,
Makes you look bad,
Sometimes it need to be pointed out.
I love you,
Always will unconditionally,
No matter what.
I hope you read this,
I hope you know,
You still mean so much to me.

What Is Love?

From all of these experiences,

The struggles I've been through,

I have no clue anymore on what love is.

Everyone has their own perspective on love,

And what love truly means to them,

Thoughts like these never came in mind.

Today these days it's more of expecting things,

More than the other differences,

Like trust, intelligence, humbleness, loyalty, and respect.

People now care about useless things that's wrong,

How many people they had sex with,

Or to a couple if they have *"done it"* yet.

To add with what rap songs include in today's society,

Having a main chick or side hoes & that stupidity,

Which is horrid in so many cases.

I feel like this generation doesn't know what love is,

I don't think they'd truly know what **LOVE** is,

Even though it maybe complicated it's hard to define.

That Certain Feeling

Have you ever felt something in your heart that seems so relieving? Something that you can be proud to say? Trials that I've experienced in my life, there's moments where I was proud with the decisions & choices. Standing up for what I personally believe makes me into the person I am today. The individuals, good & bad, made an impact in my life for the better. People might be haters & say hurtful things about who I am, but all of the negativity doesn't mean a certain thing to me. Yes, I am indeed proud of who I'm becoming. There maybe mess ups along the way. There will be complications & breaking moments along the way. Taking risks, and doing what makes me happy. What I'm doing with writing is making me happy. It's what I enjoy, and it's what I love to do.

Bestfwand

Dedication: To my bestfwand, Jessica White, she has been there for me through thick & thin, and we always have a blast when we do get the chance to hang out! I love you Jessica, this is for you!

This chick,
Words can't even describe
our bond,
We are inseparable,
She's like my older sister,
My partner-in-crime,
The ride or die type of girl,
We've been through so
much,
She's such a strong girl,
And I love her for it,
We always have a blast,
I can be myself around her,
Weirdos all around,
But that's okay,
Because we both LOVE
being weird,
She has impacted my life
for the better,
And I'm glad that she's in
my life,
Because I have NO idea
what I'd do without her,
I love you bestfwand,
Forever & always!

I want to take the time to say a massive thank you for the ones who believed in me and wanted me to continue writing. I want to thank my family for the endless support, and my friends back at home for supporting me!

I especially want to thank my two teachers who made me love writing even more. Mrs. Vennes & Ms. Schmitz, thank you for helping me to become better at writing & expand the way I write. Thank you for inspiring me to do something I absolutely love! Thank you as well to my old high school principal, Mr. Bell for as well giving me the motivation to continue on writing! I also want to thank my Senior Project teacher, Mr. Tucker! He also got me motivated to write continuously more!

I just want to say an overall thank you, and I hope to bring more into the future!

- Denise Kollock

Lightning Source UK Ltd.
Milton Keynes UK
UKRC010245030619
343637UK00008B/92